Soft Riot

TAHIR HUSSAIN

Dedicated to my Instagram Family for consistently showering your love
and support.

I continue to write because of you all.

Love,
Tahir

CONTENTS

Join me in this riot of words,
For the soft part of your souls.

For the Generation

This generation is an expert on "who cares less"

And trust me—

We do it with finesse.

This generation taught us to keep words repressed

And mail all your emotions to an empty address

This generation taught us

To deal with coldness with coldness

Until it's winter for all

And everyone freezes

You didn't want love

You just wanted the next high

Bigger than the last one

We live in times

Where the poor don't know hunger

The beautiful feel ugly

The loud are considered wise

And the wise held in contempt

The fulfilled feel empty

And the empty, *content.*

Most people these days

Seem like an Insta bio

A LinkedIn post

A bumble caption

A tweet

A contact that you can delete

Directionless hearts,

Wandering with broken compasses.

The curse of this generation—

To touch, love and flirt,

Yet be shaped by hurt.

All I see are hearts undecided

If they want to submit or rebel

Craving both, achieving neither

Chasing grass that's always greener

A society cheering innocence's demise

It's like we went forward in time

But backward in being wise

Courting most now is courting chaos itself

Courting most now is nothing but loss

Unless, you're courting yourself

My city is not the destination

My city is a stepping stone

Trust me, I've been here since I was born.

My city is your first job, your college,

Your first relationship, your first company
Whether you join it or build it

My city is built on concrete and code
Asia's Silicon Valley

Million-dollar-funded startups

Entrepreneurs in every alley
The traffic here might be a crawl
But life here never feels like it's stalled.

My city loves to brew
Both coffee and beer
My city loves to drink
My city doesn't snow
But wait till it's summer – And she bathes in pink

My city brings in people in numbers
It's not hard to understand

Simply put, my city is what young India desperately demands.

What would we do with all that *wealth,*

When our cars are only going to end up stuck in traffic?

What would we do with all that *freedom,*

When love is rare and non-existent,

But sex is easy and quick?

What would we do with all these *people,* flooding my city in scores

When friendships seem distant,

And loneliness is the only thing that knocks on my doors?

What world are we creating

If we find it difficult in simply

Breathing.

He loved working

He loved making money

He loved whiskey at the bar

He loved his pals

He loved his own life

He loved his space

He loves food but he hates cooking

He loved sex

He used the apps sometimes

But nobody stayed over after noon

The only twist here is—

He isn't really a he.

It's a she.

And it's 2023.

A salute to all my ladies.

Imagine a war on its way

And the king was busy entertaining himself and chasing all the women in his kingdom.

It's a mad world.

I feel like I've never been married once,

But I've been divorced twice.

It's a mad world.

People come,

And bring all their people in your mind,

And leave nothing but heavy stories of faceless characters behind.

It's a mad world.

Between creation and consumption,

We're blurring the lines of addiction.

It's a mad world.

We don't call it baggage anymore,

But trauma; now we wear it like a badge of honor.

It's a mad world.

We don't say fuck buddy anymore,

But situationships.

Because food is not the only thing we get delivered in 30 minutes

But we like our lovers too—

On our fingertips.

Let them ghost,

Don't expect courageous actions out of a coward's heart.

Let them ghost.

How can they tell you how they feel,

When they don't even know themselves?

Let them ghost.

Let them feel the awkwardness when they see you in a social setting.

Not you. Never you.

Let them ghost.

For everyone leaving their tier 2 cities for tier 1,

Thinking the dating pool is unlimited.

How poorly you judge,

You'll run out of people sooner than you think,

Like running out of the city's water itself—the very water we drink.

Let them ghost.

And then maybe lurk in your stories like the sorry shameful creatures they really are.

Let them ghost.

Every ghosting is a reminder for you to go deeper in yourself and your life.

Let them ghost.

Because this truth I'll impart,

Even when they'd meet their perfect match,

In a perfect start,

They'd want nothing more than one night.

Because ghosting is nothing but their way of rebelling against their own bodies and hearts.

Let them ghost.

When you wake up one day and see their empty display pictures.

Know that 'empty' was their soul too.

Isn't it easy to play without the heart?

The games have no stakes.

When nothing is real, nothing breaks?

Traffic crawled,

Dogs barked.

Rats scurried around—

Under the flyover,

On Outer Ring Road,

Next to an alcohol shop.

A PPT sent,

Inside a cab.

Trolleys rolled for a new tenant,

A pothole avoided.

Money moved between accounts,

Creating questionable value.

The kids partied to a new Bollywood song.

And my city—

Continued to hum along.

Easy to fall in love with,

Hard to love.

In 2025

Tech bankrupted our morals

In a world where we chase digital thrones

Comedy became political

And dignity left our bones

We upgraded our organs every 3 years

Our organs now our phones

It's only a matter of time

Until AI makes our clones

So we did what we did best

We turned to our god

And made money our goal

Because what else was security,

In this twisted little black hole?

While the poets simply watched on

Playing doctors to our souls.

Love

I want to tattoo

My love on your skin,

With kisses.

Leave hickeys,

Like a hot brand.

While you wear my words,

Like a piercing on your soul.

She was a simple breeze

On a hot summer's day.

She was a glimpse of the moon

On a cloudy night.

She was the kindness of a stranger.

She was color to a blind man's sight

Love with a force

Of a hundred volcanoes

Simmering,

Yet gentle—

Like a butterfly's flap.

I was mostly quiet with my thoughts,

Usually keeping them to myself.

But with her,

"What are you thinking?" she would ask,

Innocently, looking up at me with those big anime eyes—

Like she's casting a spell I can't escape.

Making my lips move on their own,

Spilling all my entrails.

Smooth jazz & smoother wine

A woman who loves my lines,

An evening with all the time, to converse and dine.

Monogamy, but filled with passion.

Orgasms on repeat.

Eyes and hands for no other, but mine.

Private, no lying,

No hype and definitely no swipes.

Stack the bread, while I come home to her in bed.

Bed and Breakfast

Between your legs.

I like the spread,

But what I like more are all those pretty thoughts in her head

Just leaving verses —For a love that's sacred

When you love a woman,

Love the *wolf* in her too.

Because the wolf in her is rabid and feral, Tumultuously, a rebel.

She likes to claw and be bitten,

Best not to be smitten.

The wolf in her,

Is a lover of all things forbidden.

No time for indecision—

As she beckons you closer.

Be advised,

To leave behind all tradition.

Something protective inside you

Speaks to that something protective inside of me.

And that language doesn't need any words at all.

Blazed in a blazer,

And a bralette that shimmered.

No makeup,

But she still managed to glitter.

Attitude backed up those looks,

But I bet she'd differ.

It was a hot summer night,

And her eyes sent shivers.

She was a lover, a fighter,

A princess from the land of the five rivers.

And as she drew in closer—

Looks like tonight I'll be…

Having dessert,

Before dinner.

It hurts when she does it first.

It hurts every month.

It hurts beyond belief when she gives birth.

It hurts when she follows all those beauty routines.

It hurts when she loves—

As if her flesh speaks the language of pain.

Even without nature having to explain.

So in between these hurts, let's love her as much as we can.

Not because we're chivalrous or gentlemen,

But just because we're humane.

I'm sorry I couldn't step up

Every time you asked for something stable

I'm sorry I was the variable

When you were the constant

You were the light on my good days and the bad nights

I'm sorry we never made music,

When our heartbeats were *already in consonance.*

You'll know with my touch—

I don't want to conquer you,

But play with you, like equals on this field.

You'll know with my touch,

This love isn't a cage, but an embrace.

From hands that once held swords,

Now forming a shield.

You'll know with my touch,

Every fingertip, a melody untold,

For music waiting—

On dusty instrumentals of your soul.

Inside every man is a warrior—

Who will bleed for his woman.

Who will lay down his life for his love.

Who will scale mountains and swim oceans.

Who will walk miles—

Just for a smile.

And inside every woman is a little girl—

Who wants just that.

A princess who wants to feel safe,

Protected at all costs.

Someone who will journey the desert,

Back to her—no matter how far.

Someone she trusts with her body and her heart.

You see, we were made perfect,

We just didn't come with an instruction manual.

So, we listened to fears,

We listened to peers.

We planted doubts,

Because those voices were louder

Than the ever-present tug at our hearts.

It was night, the waves thundered.

They crashed into a rock—

One after the other.

The beach washed up,

The flimsy huts vanished,

The tourists vacated.

Everything that could fall, fell.

Everything that could leave, left.

But the rock stood.

The ocean was misunderstood.

The ocean raged,

And the rock became its calm.

And come morning,

None but the rock bore witness—

To how serene the ocean could be.

How she playfully shimmered.

The dance of

The ocean being a lover,

And the rock its mistress.

I'm hoping you have a spark inside you,

One that refuses to be put out.

I'm hoping you love like a 90s kid— Old school throughout.

I'm hoping kindness is your first language,

And your native tongue.

I'm hoping your love is so strong,

That I'll definitely get drunk.

I'm hoping you don't treat love like a game,

And no matter how much you've been hurt—

You'll never cause someone pain.

I'm hoping you love and live fearlessly,

And have the courage to take a chance.

And even when we're surrounded by

Thunderstorms and heatwaves—

You're still willing to dance.

I'm hoping you'll be my safe space,

In a world caught in a race.

I'm hoping you'll put in the effort, fight, communicate.

I'm hoping this right swipe isn't too late.

The quickest way to my heart is the long route.

You know, where we stay friends first.

Where we're not acting on all our crazy hormones and thirst.

The quickest way to my heart is closed off.

Why would you take shortcuts—

Am I not worth the effort?

The quickest way to my heart is for you to know

How flawed I am.

And for me to know

How flawed you are.

Then we take time and decide—

Do we give this a go,

Or stay far apart?

The quickest way to my heart will take you eons—

Because it took me all my life to find.

And if you're still here reading,

And need an answer—

Then take these three words:

Just be kind.

We'll get along if you manage to bear my midnight snores.

We'll get along if we can amicably split the house chores.

We'll get along if we go Dutch more often than not.

We'll get along if, as shallow as it seems, together we look hot.

We'll get along if you pick my call and I pick yours

On a hectic Wednesday, when you're having a bad one.

And I understand with just a hey.

We'll get along if my cat, Gigi, likes you—

And Gigi doesn't like anyone.

We'll get along if you're as fun as you seem.

We'll get along if

You accept my shortcomings and I accept yours,

And we don't pull each other's strings.

We'll get along if you believe in your intuition and feeling.

Because I have a feeling,

We'll get along.

Hurt

It was bad when you were making excuses

It was worse

When I was doing it for you.

You were unhealthy for your own self

How could I possibly think

You would be healthy for me.

Letting you go was easy

Because you were never really there to begin with.

Letting you go was easy

Because you gave me all the reasons to.

Now when I look behind—

I jumped into you with blinds.

It hurt,

But not when I let you go—

But when the curtains of the real you opened with time.

You know why it hurts so bad?
Because you gave away your best self—
the one you built proudly.

The one where you loved courageously.
The one where you believed naively.
You gave your best self,

thinking it would be enough.

And when it was not,
you were left standing, wondering
if any of you was worthy at all.

You see, that's the power of love.
It can make you or break you.

And for that soul who was broken—
you were always enough.
You are more than enough,
more than you can possibly think.

You are millennia's perfection.
There was nothing to fix.
Be proud that you loved with no tricks.
You are a sum greater than all your inner conflicts.

You are water—water to thirsty lips.
You are water, and they were oil.

You just didn't mix.

I don't feel I can love anyone like I loved you.

You came in at a time when my body was young,

My ideals intact.

You fucked my lust away.

I loved you so much,

That in fact, I learned to love myself more.

And when you hurt—

The blood rushed back to my brain.

I saw the pain.

I saw it all—

The patterns.

The mistakes.

The meaningless keepsakes.

I threw them all away.

Happy face makeup,

Hiding ugly broken scars.

Bright red lehengas,

Hiding sad blue hearts.

He had a steady wage and was rejected

He then bought a shop and was rejected

He then bought a farm and was rejected

He then bought the mines and was rejected

He then bought a kingdom and then rejected them all.

I burned my fingers loving you.

And when I healed,

I realized—

I craved the heat more than

Feeling nothing at all.

Being with you taught me to love myself,

Because you so prudently did.

Being with you taught me kindness,

Because with you, that virtue was almost always off the grid.

Being with you taught me what I really wanted and deserved,

Which, previously I could barely admit.

Being with you taught me—

That people not only lie to others,

But few, to themselves too.

You measure lost loves—

Not by the time you spent with them,

But by the intensity you felt.

I wanted to be your palace

I wanted to entertain all your friends

I wanted to throw loving feasts for your family

I wanted to show camaraderie to your colleagues

But

You just wanted me in an isolated room,

A lover closed off in four walls to fulfil all your needs

I wanted to be your palace.

They said, "Feel all your feelings till they're no more"

So, I felt the sadness till my tears dried,

I felt the anger till my knuckles bruised,

But love, what about love?

What could I do with that?

On breakups

A wise girl once told me

Love can happen many times in life

But real effort – *Just once*

Love waits.

Waits for that one day—

When that person will step up,
When that person will change.

We give it all,
Thinking that one day,
That person will be
Everything you want them to be.

And when that day never comes—

The love that waits,

Breaks.

And everything with it

Dissipates.

You were my early mornings,

You were my late nights,

You were my afternoon delight,

You were all my adoration,

You were my muse,

And for you,

Nothing I'd refuse.

Nothing to repress.

So much to express.

I loved you in excess.

Because you were my Goddess

But now, you are a lost memory.

Your words lost in frequency,

You are the one that got away,

The one that I'd never want back.

You were once all the colours combined,

But now, here, stands nothing but black.

You are the high that I'll never want back

You left promises — broken

You were a forbidden door

I never thought I'd open

My only sin is that I saw all your darkness and still loved you the most.

You were my Goddess, or were you?

You were my Goddess, *once.*

You were my Goddess, once.

And now you will forever remain a ghost.

Loving your darkness,

Cost me my own light.

She said she wanted to explore everything,

Experience everything.

That included me

I wish someone, somewhere told her

I was a human being —

Not an experience.

The only thing *worse*
Than a broken heart —

Is shattered idealism.

Like every addiction—

I only fell out of love

When the pain of being with you,

Was greater than the pleasure of being with you.

Healing

.

This soul is a library of stories.

Come take a read.

Sit down.
Get comfortable.
Pick out the pages—

But take them with you tonight.

Because these stories are too heavy,

And this soul—too light.

And that's the purpose of the broken, isn't it?

To heal—

And not to break everything and everyone else further?

And the words,

They came all at once,

And they stopped all at once.

The only variable in this equation was *you.*

My angels couldn't get through to you,

Because you let your demons guard your heart.

Winter's first shade.

Do you feel it in the sky?

Do you hear it in the tune?

Winter's first shade.

Out of complete nothingness,

A new flower blooms.

Like the earth needed nothing,
And the soul needed nothing,

But itself.

Winter's first shade.

We have left behind the monsoon,

We have left behind sure -shot doom.

Winter's first shade.

A new season looms.

I'm too old now—

For the games women play.

To be the focus of your group chat for a few days,
Or the content for your dreary life.

To be your first—
Or to be your last.

To be someone you had a new experience with,
A summer fling—
Or someone
For whom you once had a thing.

See, I know how it ends.

I know how long your attention span is.

I know why you do what you do—

I see the dirt under the carpet that you never seem to look.

I know these feelings come with an expiration date,
Or a slight inconvenience,
Or when the newness fades.

I'm too old now—

And these games have lost their charm.

I've been mentioned in more group chats than I can count,

And more rooms at midnight—

Where my name was once announced.

So, keep your five-minute attention—

For the boys who are younger.

Take your tequila shots for the night,
Look pretty, dress in style.

And keep walking—

When you see the fine wine aisle.

And the strongest of winds can move the
widest of clouds,
And the smallest of rains can quench the
driest of deserts.

What's a broken heart that some self-love
can't fix?

Keep the door open,

The ones who want to stay will stay.

Keep your home clean,

The ones who do not respect it, can leave.

The walls you build,

Are not walls on the inside.

But on the outside,

They hide how beautiful you really are

Or can be

And when I say beautiful—

I don't mean looks at all

I was full enough to love you,

I was foolish enough to believe you,

And when push came to shove,

I was brave enough to leave you.

Pink sunsets

Purple skies

Green lands

Black hearts—

Attempting white love.

I was stupid,

To think that walking out from you would be my doom

I was stupid,

Because walking out from you, was my bloom, baby.

My bloom.

Forgetting you

was remembering

Who I was.

I wish I could tell my younger self,

You'll get to an age,

Where looks and kinks won't be sexy.

Efforts will turn you on,

And that's the best phase yet.

If you find patterns in your life repeating

It just means you've not grown from your mistakes

The universe is trying to teach you.

Kindness is the escalator to my proximity

The kinder you are,

The closer you will get to me

Regardless of gender, religion, sexuality, location, age, wealth or status.

And the more heartless you are,

Regardless of looks, connections and influence.

The further you will be away from me.

That's a value carved in stone,

Just something about me to be known.

Dear Brother

I know your first crush was a hurt you'll spend the rest of your life fixing.

I hope someone tells you that you're worth it. That you matter.

I wish the world wasn't so cruel and your emotions, a laughing matter.

Dear Brother

I wish you get the girl you love.

I know you'd do anything to keep her happy.

Even at the cost of yourself.

I wish the fantasies you have in your head, happen.

I wish you feel the happiness of being in a home full of love,

And you're the centre of attention.

Dear Brother

You suffer so much in silence.

An ocean deep, turned mute.

A mountain on your back

And up ahead, a crooked track.

A world turned upside down

And morals out of whack.

These branches that you battle

Have too many thorns.

And your sword, wearing thin.

Yet you're expected to do nothing but win.

Dear Brother

I wish I could give you rest.

I wish you, your parents' embrace

I wish to see your happiest face

I wish to see you with no worries

I wish you go through life with no hurries

Dear Brother

Our blood forked long ago with our ancestors

And our souls split long before that

We never shared a womb

Or a meal

I don't know your name

But whenever I see you, I know what you feel.

Dear Brother

I hope you never lose your charm

All those things that make you, you.

I hope you never lose your light.

I'm rooting for you

That you never go down without a fight

I know the universe steals you off your glow

Every turn it gets

And just like the universe

You are its son

I hope the universe doesn't forget

And only you choose when you set

Art

Poets are just mortals

Who have touched God with their fingertips.

Every chip to my work

Was a chip at my soul.

Every strike making art,

I finally understand what Picasso meant

When he said

Art was chaos taking shape.

Almost all of us had all the senses,

But when beauty sprung,

Only the Poets wrote.

The Artists drew.

And the Musicians sung.

I am a poet,

And I didn't belong to one woman,

I belonged to the divine feminine.

And she was everyone,

And no one at the same time.

I felt out of place at open mics,

Like a jock in a room full of nerds.

The one who actually tasted euphoria,

In a room wishing sorely they did too.

Sometimes I feel like

I'm the violin for the universe

Only a violin knows the pain it must take to make sweet music for others.

And just like the violin, I want my strings pushed to their limits and exhausted by the time my time is up.

Every piece of poem I wrote

Left my soul lighter.

I now know why the Egyptians

After they wither,

Measured their hearts against a feather.

I've learnt the secret of writing beautifully

Is thinking beautifully.

Death & Purpose

I have tallied my own death,

So don't seat me next to mortal men.

Who talk about anything, but their mortal wealth
With their mortal problems,

Wasting, their mortal breath.

My chessboard

Just had a king.

And I still learned to win.

The warrior won the war,

And a king was born.

The king leads the people,

And a sage was born.

The sage taught,

And a generation was born.

If you know you're going to die in the next 15 months

And there is absolutely nothing wrong in the way you are living and what you are doing right now.

Then you are on your Purpose.

Knowing your purpose is knowing God himself.

To stand at his feet at heaven's gates,

To know and navigate both realms physical and ethereal.

The Red of my fire

Asks me to be hedonistic

It asks me to ragingly consume

The entire forest itself

For satisfying nothing but my appetite

The Red of my fire

Asks me to destroy

Ruthlessly anything that might oppose me

The Red of my fire

Is for every bit of my body

It is ambition in all its dirty glory.

The Red of my fire

Is nothing but unrest

It asks me to leave nothing

But ashes for the rest

The Blue of my fire

Infinitely ~~consumes~~ creates

The Blue of my fire

Ignites in prayer

In ~~chaos~~ focus

In ~~violence~~ silence

In ~~public~~ solitude

The Blue of my fire

Is not to burn, but to elevate

The engine that propels others

It asks me to ignite every soul that comes into its contact

The Blue of my fire

Asks me to forgive,

Purging parts of myself.

The Blue of my fire

Asks not what it can take,

But what it can give.

The Blue of my fire

Is not of this realm

It is the gift of the sages, old.

And all the truth that needs to be told.

The Blue of my fire

Is wisdom incarnate

It intuitively knows

The Blue of my fire

Is the ~~roar~~ whisper

Of a thousand unstoppable infernos

Most people plunder the earth,

Not concerned about the tomorrows.

Most people plunder souls,

Not concerned about the tomorrows.

Few people plant seeds in this earth,

For the harvest of tomorrow.

Few people plant seeds in souls,

For the bloom of tomorrow.

When you're selfless,

When you're on your purpose.

When you're vibrating at the highest frequency,

It's funny, how the universe itself becomes your genie.

Purpose can't be selfish,

It must be beyond yourself.

It is the middle point where you meet the universe itself and shake
its hands.

That's the thing about the soul

You can twist the arm,

But you can never break the spirit

You can grab the throat but you can never choke it

You can shut the mouth but you can never mute it

You can execute a genocide but you can never win it

How can you bomb away

 resolve? How can you stab faith?

How can you grenade love?

That's the thing about the soul

The inertia of pleasure is so strong

That only the gravity of purpose can pull you away from it.

I want to howl with the wolves

I want to hunt with the tigers

I want to swim with the sharks

I want to enamor virgin hearts and fill them with my seed

I want the sharp edge of an axe on my chest

When I'm not backing down

I will bleed

For my land and my home and my cause

Tell me, I'm not the only one who feels this ache in his balls?

This world will bury itself in riches, debt and toys.

Sell their soul for empty tomorrows,

And then travel away from their surroundings just to see what's within.

Leave me to my words,

Leave me to my art.

The world will revel,

At all of my youthful rebellions.

Long after I'm gone

Remembering how

The divine and the devil,

Danced in one vessel.

Life is a baton passed to you.

Every generation—running as fast, hard, and long as possible,
So they can pass the baton to the next.

The struggle. The war. The famines.
The sickness. The superstitions. The depression.

And when death came knocking at their door,
They shooed it away—
Because they had to run further, for you.

A millennia's struggle in your DNA,
Blood spilled for our country.
Sweat dripped for its welfare.
Tears flowed in the fight—

For the hope of tomorrow,
For today,
For you.

Shoulders that needed rest, but kept pushing.
Hands that didn't have water to clean themselves—
Yet still held our mother's mother.

Mouths that went uneaten for their sons.
Eyes that never saw our OLED screens,
Ears that never listened to our music.

Hearts that could never roam as freely as we do now.

And legs—

Legs that never stopped, for you.

So we could be where we are today,

Life is a baton passed to you.

Do not question it.

Do not take it for granted.
Do not wallow.

We are the sum of a million tomorrows.

And what we do now—
Will affect a million more.

What remains,

When you've had all the pleasure?

When you've played with all the toys?

When you've gauged all minds?

What remains,

But humility and service?

"When do you think you will stop writing?",
they asked.

"When do you think I'll stop *feeling?*", I asked back.

When I Die

Celebrate my funeral, joyously. Invite everybody.

And ask everyone to bring along

The words and poems I engraved on their hearts,

On pieces of papers, to put them in my grave.

And then let's see,

If the 6 feet they dug

Holds my words more

Or if it holds more mud.

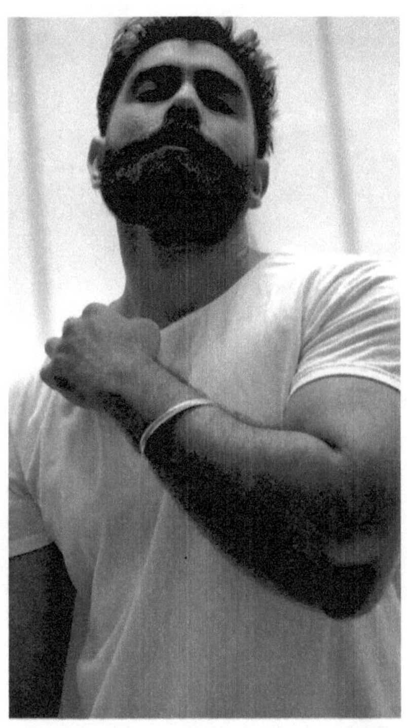

Tahir Hussain (born 23 November 1992, Bangalore, India) is a celebrated Indian poet known for his evocative and concise style of writing. His poetry, which gained widespread recognition on Instagram, delves into themes of passionate love, the dualities of life, and the rapidly shifting ideologies of India's digital "swipe" generation.

Blending heartfelt observations with a modern perspective, Tahir's work resonates deeply with readers navigating the evolving intersections of technology, relationships, and identity in contemporary India.

www.ingramcontent.com/pod-product-compliance
Lightning Source LLC
Chambersburg PA
CBHW031300130726
47988CB00007B/2654